MW01615572

The Lady of the Wheel

(La Ruotaia)

Library of Congress Cataloging-in-Publication Data

Coniglio, Angelo F.
   The lady of the wheel : (La Ruotaia) / Angelo F. Coniglio.
     p. cm. -- (Sicilian studies ; v. 23)
   ISBN 1-881901-86-6 (pbk.)
   1. Sicily (Italy)--Social life and customs--Fiction. I. Title.
   PS3603.O5336R8613 2012
   813'.6--dc23

                 2012010405

Acknowledgments

Cover design by Ronald C. Coniglio
Cover photo of the *Chiesa Madre Racalmuto* by Ennio Demori.

For information and for orders, write to:
LEGAS

P.O. Box 149
Mineola, New York
11501, USA

3 Wood Aster Bay
Ottawa, Ontario
KIN 8T9 Canada

www.Legaspublishing.com
Printed in Canada

Angelo F. Coniglio

The Lady of the Wheel
(La Ruotaia)

LEGAS

Legas
Sicilian Studies
Volume XXIII

Series Editor: Gaetano Cipolla

Other Volumes Published in this Series:

1. Giuseppe Quatriglio, *A Thousand Years in Sicily: from the Arabs to the Bourbons*, transl. by Justin Vitiello, 1992, 1997;
2. Henry Barbera, *Medieval Sicily: the First Absolute State*, 1994, 2000;
3. Connie Mandracchia DeCaro, *Sicily, the Trampled Paradise, Revisited*, 1998; 2008;
4. Justin Vitiello, *Labyrinths and Volcanoes: Windings Through Sicily*, 1999;
5. Ben Morreale, *Sicily: The Hallowed Land*, 2000;
6. Joseph Privitera, *The Sicilians*, 2001;
7. Franco Nicastro and Romolo Menighetti, *History of Autonomous Sicily*, transl. by Gaetano Cipolla, 2002;
8. Maria Rosa Cutrufelli, *The Woman Outlaw*, transl. by Angela M. Jeannet, 2004;
9. Enzo Lauretta, *The Narrow Beach*, transl. by Giuliana Sanguinetti Katz and Anne Urbancic, 2004;
10. Venera Fazio and Delia De Santis, ed. *Sweet Lemons: Writings with a Sicilian Accent*, 2004;
11. *The Story of Sicily*, 2005. (Never printed);
12. Gaetano Cipolla, *Siciliana: Studies on the Sicilian Ethos*, 2005;
13. Paolo Fiorentino, *Sicily Through Symbolism and Myth*, 2006;
14. Giacomo Pilati, *Sicilian Women*, transl. by Anthony Fragola, 2008;
15. *Prayers and Devotional Songs of Sicily*, ed. & transl. by Peppino Ruggeri. 2009.
16. Giovanna Summerfield & John Shelly Summerfield, Jr., *Remembering Sicily*, 2009.
17. Joseph Cacibauda, *After Laughing Comes Crying: Sicilian Immigrants on Louisiana Plantations*, 2009;
18. Domenico Tempio, *Poems and Fables*, transl by G. Summerfield, 2010.
19. *Sweet Lemons 2: International Writings with a Sicilian Accent*, ed. by V. Fazio and D. DeSantis, 2010.
20. Giuseppe Quatriglio, *Sicily: Island of Myths*, transl. by Florence Russo and Gaetano Cipolla, 2011.
21. *First to Last Picking: Sicilians in America: Yesterday, Today, Tomorrow*, by Sebastiano Santostefano, 2011.Y
22. *La Terra di Babele, Saggi sul plurilinguismo nella cultura italiana*, a cura di D. Brancato e M. Ruccolo, 2011.

Dedication

In memory of my parents Rosa Alessi and Gaetano Coniglio of Serradifalco, Province of Caltanissetta, Sicily, who left everything to establish a family in the new world. To my wife Angie and my son Angelo, both full-blooded Sicilians, and in memory of another, my own dark-haired, green-eyed daughter Angela.

Table of Contents

Foreword 9

PROLOGUE 11

Chapter 1. 13

Chapter 2. 21

Chapter 3. 25

Chapter 4. 29

Chapter 5. 35

Chapter 6. 41

Chapter 7. 45

Chapter 8. 51

Chapter 9. 55

Chapter 10. 59

Chapter 11. 65

Chapter 12. 71

Chapter 13. 75

Chapter 14. 79

Foreword

This story is about late-1800's Sicily, which had only recently been under the yoke of Spanish Bourbon rule. Though feudalism had been nominally abolished in 1812, its customs and social restrictions were still felt.

I have used some phrases in the Sicilian language, translated when necessary. The Sicilian convention of names is also followed. Thus, Maria Rizzo, though married to Antonino Alessi, keeps her surname, but her children have the surname Alessi. Their oldest children's given names are derived from those of Antonino and Maria's parents.

The work is fiction, but the place names are real. The personal names are typical of the region, as are the customs alluded to, and the choices made for the names of foundlings.

Although it appears in no modern Italian dictionary and it is unfamiliar to even well-educated Italians, the word *ruotaia* was used regularly in the public records of Sicily at the time of this story, in the context explained herein. Other archaic words are used, and are either translated or self-explanatory. An actual person with the name and occupation of the protagonist in this story once lived in Racalmuto, Agrigento Province, Sicily. Beyond that, the fictional person by that name bears no relation to the actual person, and none is intended. I thank the real *ruotaia* for the inspiration to write this story.

Angelo F. Coniglio
January 7, 2010

PROLOGUE

Sicily has a history as old as man. It attained its golden age in the time of the Saracens and the Normans, from about 800 through 1200 AD. But since then, *"La Bedda Sicilia"* has struggled under the yoke of one oppressor after another, causing its common folk to bear famine, hardship and poverty.

A harsh reflection of that poverty is seen in the stories of the foundlings of Sicily in the seventeenth, eighteenth and nineteenth centuries, when starving parents were often forced to abandon newborns in order to be able to care for their other children. In the town of Racalmuto, in the year 1869 there were a total of six hundred twenty-one births recorded. Eighty of those infants, more than ten percent, were foundlings, left in *la ruota*, the 'foundling wheel' of the church.

The abandoned children sometimes were left in rags (*involti nelle fascie* – literally, 'wrapped in swaddling clothes'), but often they were dressed in fine clothes of linen and wool, with colorful embroidery and lace. Records of births were surprisingly well-documented in nineteenth century Sicily, and a record was made for every child born, whether of legitimate parents, or left in 'the wheel'. These records usually showed that the child's father presented the baby to a town official for the recording of the birth. The record typically gave the name, age, occupation and address of the father and the name of the mother, as well as the name given to the child.

But in the case of foundlings, the baby was presented to the official by the person who had taken it from the wheel; invariably a woman, called in some towns the *ricevitrice dei proietti*, the 'receiver of castoffs'. This woman gave the official the details of finding the child, and the clothes the baby was found in, all documented in the written record. Since the parents were unknown, the child was given both a first name *and* a surname by a priest or a town official.

Foundlings' surnames were intentionally stigmatic, like *Proietto* (castoff), *Esposto* (exposed), or *Trovatello* (foundling); or derisive, like *Fieramusca* (horsefly). Even when more conventional surnames were given, they were 'strange' for the town in which they were given. Thus, Coniglio is a perfectly good Sicilian surname, but if there was no family by that name in the town where a foundling was named Giovanni Coniglio, everyone in town knew that the child was a foundling (and thus assumed to be a bastard). Today, such naming practices might well be considered child abuse.

Chapter 1.

Racalmuto is an ancient city in the southwest of Sicily, in the old province of Girgenti, some miles north of the Mediterranean Sea. The town was already old in 830 AD, when conquering Saracens called it *'Rahal Maut'*, the ruined city. It was even more ancient by 1869, just a few years after Garibaldi had 'unified' Sicily with the Kingdom of Italy, driving out the Spanish Bourbons. From the time of dominance of the Saracen Moors, through the oppression of the Italians, the island had been ruled successively by Normans, Germans, and the French. Then, for more than half a millennium, it had endured a long decline under the yoke of the Aragonese and their successors, the Bourbons. Surviving the more recent masters, the fabric of the town retained its Moorish and Norman influences.

Women wore black or dark, loose fitting clothes, and wore shawls to obscure their faces. They might walk through the streets, but only with groups of other women. Lone women were never to be seen outside their home. After age seven or eight, boys and girls were strictly segregated.

Still maintaining their medieval style, the streets were of stone, as were the buildings along their narrow courses. In some seasons, stone buildings may have a desirable effect: as the seasons warm up, the cool stone can alleviate the heat inside a dwelling. In fall, the stone captures the sun's lessening warmth and holds it thru the night. But in the dead of winter, when the sun is weak and stingy with its energy, the air is cold, the stone seems even colder, and the walls suck the heat out of the living spaces. Acknowledging this fact of nature,

Sicilian builders had long ago begun to build residences on a simple vertical formula: the ground floor held a family's stock of animals, such as they could afford. The next floor, called the *primo piano*, was a common room used for cooking, eating, and daily life, and the next floor provided a sleeping area. In this way, the warm, if somewhat pungent, body heat of the animals rose to the living quarters, where it combined with the heat of the cooking fire to warm the sleeping area above.

But it was *very* cold, that winter of 1869 in Racalmuto. Families without several beasts, or too poor to keep a fire going, could almost feel their own body heat fleeing through the stone walls. In one of the stone row-houses, Maria Rizzo sat cross-legged, avoiding the outside walls in a corner of the sleeping room. She shared the room with her husband Antonino Alessi and their children Totò, Grazia, Tanuzzu, and two-year-old Giuseppa. It was early morning, and in spite of the cold, she was sweating profusely.

Maria was sweating because she had just given birth. And because the infant had lived.

Nino Alessi had been out of the house for some time, at his job as a *picuneri*, a pickman in the local sulfur mine. As usual, he had left an hour before dawn in the rickety mule-drawn *carrozza* that hauled the men from the town to the mine and back. He would return long after the sun had gone down. Their other thin, curly-topped children had murmured and squirmed while Maria was in the throes of labor, but thankfully, none had awakened.

Now Maria looked at the newborn girl and asked herself "Why did I bathe and dress her? I'm going to throw her into the river, after all." She had told Nino the lie that the fetus was dead, that it hadn't moved for a week. He was resigned to the fact. Secretly, he had thought it a blessing.

Antonino had worked at the mine for years. The wages, though a pittance, were normally more than he could earn as a share-cropper. But with the recent drought and its spawn, famine, more and more *contadini* had forsaken the plow and taken up the pick. Wages at the mine had plummeted. The lone, scraggly milk goat they kept on the ground floor below their humble living quarters had virtually dried up, and it was harder and harder to find food, even if he could afford it. Having another mouth to feed would have been disastrous.

Maria knew this as well as Nino. That was why she had lied about the baby being dead. Soon Totò would be seven. Old enough to work at the mine as a *carusu*, lugging baskets of sulfur ore, dug up by the pickmen, from the depths of the mine to its mouth. That would bring more money to the family, since the mine bosses would soon come around to offer the *succursu di murti*, the "death benefit" for Totò. They would pay Antonino a few *scuti*, and Totò would go: to work, live, eat and sleep in the mine until he died, or a miracle happened -- he might prove worthy someday to become a pickman like his father, and work in the mine only from dawn until dusk.

Maria's heartbreak over Totò's impending fate was assuaged by the prospect that the *succursu* would help, for a time, to buy food, and that Totò's share of their simple meals could be apportioned to the other children. Keeping this baby would negate those bitter advantages. And even though she had milk, Tanuzzu and Giuseppa were still breast-feeding and there was not enough for another child.

The fact of her pregnancy had been hidden through the forced lack of neighborly contact during this cold winter, as well as by the bulky clothing she normally wore. In their dark sleeping area, Nino knew, though he never saw her slim body. Once, after intimacy, he had commented, "My *Mariuzz* has grown a *panzedda*, a little belly." She told him then that she was expecting, but though she couldn't see his face in the dark, she knew from his silence that the news had not brought him joy, but rather, concern.

After Maria's dark deed had been carried out, no one must know what she had done. No, she must cast it away, or expose to be disposed of by the town's mangy dogs.

It would not be the first child she had lost. A year after her marriage, she had brought forth a baby boy, naming him Salvatore after Nino's father. But that first Totò had been sickly, and none of Maria's ministrations, nor those of the local midwife, the priest nor the town doctor could save it.

When it died at the age of three months, Maria was already pregnant, with another boy, who was born healthy and once more named Salvatore. The second boy had survived, but soon he would be given up as a *carusu*. Sicilian mothers knew of loss.

But this newborn baby was such a beautiful child, and it seemed as though Maria could see her own image in the girl's features. Black ringlets surrounded a round pink face whose cheeks were even rosier, and her remarkable green eyes pierced Maria's heart like thorns, as though the child knew of her mother's plans. Maria could not help recognizing the child's resemblance to herself, and though she knew it was vain, she thought the child, if she lived, could grow to be as attractive as she. Though her life was hard, her wiry body had still retained curvature and softness, enough to inflame her Nino, she thought.

Now she had dressed the infant in the only fine clothes the family owned, the costume of a lovely doll her father had once given her after he had returned from a visit to Palermo. A white silk hat surmounted the curls, trimmed with red velvet ribbons. A frilled white muslin shirt covered the child from neck to toe, a fine grey wool shawl swathed her shoulders, and tiny cardboard slippers, bright red, graced her feet.

Maria wrapped a threadbare cloak over her own shoulders, took up the child, and silently carried her down the stairs, past the sleeping goat, and out into the bitter cold.

She walked with her head hung in sorrow, hardly seeing where she went, through narrow cobblestone streets which seemed to merge with the stone walls of the darkened houses. She looked up and saw the signpost at a street corner: *Via Garibaldi.* She spat and crossed herself.

Garibaldi had promised that when Sicily was united with the north in an Italian republic, things would be better for the common people. Her father Gaetano Rizzo had joined with Nino's father to fight beside the *Red-shirts.* Gaetano had been wounded, and Nino's father Salvatore Alessi had died in the fight for 'unification'.

Garibaldi had won, Italy was united, but Sicily was still as poor as it had been under the recent Bourbon rule. Further, the best jobs were now taken not by local men, but by Italians from the north, and the people survived by selling their children to the mine owners.

Maria turned a corner and nearly stumbled on the lowest step of the town's Mother Church, the *Chiesa Madre Annunziata*. She caught her balance with one arm and protected the child with the other. The misstep had caused her to look up again. That was when she saw *la ruota*. The wheel was set in the wall at the side of the massive church, near the entrance to the foundlings' quarters.

She thought: "If I drown my baby, she will be a *turca*, a Turk, dying without baptism and without a soul. If I leave her in the wheel, whatever happens to her, at least she'll be christened, and have a name, and be a *cristiana*, a Christian." The leaden winter sky had brightened. Now worried that she might be seen, Maria crept along the base of the stone wall, to the niche beside the oaken 'door of the foundlings'. She sat on the cold pavement by the door, resting her back against the colder marble of the wall.

She looked at her daughter's green eyes, at the same time somehow both trusting and accusing. "At least I can give you something before I abandon you", Maria whispered, as she bared a breast for the baby to suckle. "Go ahead, go ahead, your sister will give thanks for this tomorrow."

When the baby had finished, Maria carried her to the niche. In it was set a little rotating closet, whose flat circular bottom was just large enough to hold the small bundle of life. With a tear and a heavy heart, she placed the infant on the wheel and turned it so that the baby was carried inside. She reached up and tugged a cord that shook a set of chimes within the church, then scampered away from the wheel, back through the grey streets to her house.

When she entered the living quarters, she heard Giuseppa crying, and asked "Pina, what's wrong?" The child sniffled and sobbed, *"Mamma, aiu fami!* I'm hungry!" Embracing the child, Maria cooed, "Here, here, *mammuzza,* don't cry. Here, here, I have milk."

Chapter 2.

Anna di Marco was a jovial, hearty woman who had never married. She had lived at home while her parents were alive, and learned to spin thread, weave and sew. This craft supported her for a time after they had passed, but the house then belonged to her eldest brother Lorenzo. As his family grew, the other brothers and sisters had eventually married and moved out. After Renzo's wife Concetta had borne her fourth child, it was clear to Anna that her welcome was wearing thin. She bore no malice towards her brother's wife; it was hard enough for her, with the four children. Besides her aversion to having another woman in the household, Concetta knew that the corner inhabited by Anna could provide some breathing space for her children.

Without rancor, Anna had gone to the *Chiesa Annunziata* to ask old Padre Calogero if she could help there, and he had given her a job as housekeeper, as well as a place to stay. By the time there was a young new pastor, Padre Raimondo, Anna's responsibilities had expanded to include the care of Racalmuto's orphans and foundlings. In some towns, she might have had the lofty title *Ricevitrice dei Proietti*: "Receiver of Castaways", but in Racalmuto she was known simply as *la ruotaia*, the mistress of the wheel. That cold January morning, Anna heard the chimes and hastily threw on a robe, lit a candle, and rushed down to the foundling wheel.

In it, she found a little girl, awake but quiet, peering up at her with bright green eyes. The baby's shawl had caught in the wheel, causing an opening through which the winter wind blew over her exposed face, and her cheeks were almost ruby red. The child seemed content, though, and Anna carried her up to her own cramped cubicle and laid her in a basket by the bed. She blew out the candle, and soon both the babe and the lady of the wheel were asleep.

It was one of Anna's duties to find wet-nurses for her foundlings. It sometimes happened that a mother would leave a child in the wheel, then return to say she had been pregnant and miscarried, offering to nurse a foundling for the small payment the church could afford. She could then take her "foundling" baby and be paid to nurse it. Or Anna might be able to convince a mother who was still nursing a child to take on another. She strained her memory to think whether there were any such women in town at present. There was Maria Rizzo, but no, she was still nursing two of her own. Anna would have to think of someone else. Perhaps there had been a miscarriage, or perhaps this green-eyed child's mother would return. Until such an eventuality, the orphanage wet-nurses would have to share their milk with one more baby.

Later that morning by custom and law, it was Anna's responsibility to take the infant to Padre Raimondo, the pastor, to be baptized, and then to the *municipio*, the town hall, to officially record its birth. When she arrived at the *municipio*, the mayor, Don Luigi Castiglione, who was also the town pharmacist, was beside himself. "Another one?" he asked. "This is the third one this week. You'd think the wheel would wear out!"

"Your honor," Anna asked, "Would it be better for them to be thrown into the river?"

Harumphing, the mayor indicated with an impatient gesture that Anna should get on with it. He looked out the building's front door and saw Leonardo Avenia and Giovanni Puma in their usual spot, loitering about the piazza, smoking stogies and arguing politics. "Get in here, you two, we need witnesses." To his clerk, Giuseppe Arnone, the mayor growled, "All right, *Pepe*, sharpen your quill."

After the witnesses had entered the office and were quietly standing by, Anna swore to the mayor that she had found the infant that morning in the wheel, describing the child's appearance and her clothing, which the baby still wore. Anna loosened the clothes so that the mayor could assure himself of the child's gender, and the clerk duly recorded all the pertinent information. He recorded the declarant as *"di Marco Anna, sessantacinque, ruotaia"* (Anna di Marco, age sixty-five, mistress of the wheel"). He also noted that both the child's father and her mother were *ignoti*, unknown.

Anna smiled at the mayor and said "With those red cheeks and green eyes, she has the colors of a rose, so padre Raimondo and I chose the name *Rosa* for her."

"And what of the surname? *Proietto*, thrown out, or *Gennaro*, for the month?"

"Padre Raimondo chose *Esposto*, because the child was exposed to the wind."

Don Luigi shrugged and muttered "Proietto, Esposto, Gennaro, no matter. They all mean she's a foundling. Everyone will know she's a child of sin."

Anna warily disagreed. "Your honor, we don't know that. We know only that her mother loved her enough to put her in the wheel."

"All right, all right, enough. Pepe, is it all down?

No need asking the *ruotaia* or the witnesses to sign, they haven't learned to write, since the last one. Here, let me sign."

And so it was official. The little girl with the black curls, green eyes and red cheeks, in the silk hat and the little red slippers, would thenceforth be known as Rosa Esposto.

Chapter 3.

The sulfur mine was known as *Rumpispaddi*, the Backbreaker. Hundreds of men and *carusi* worked at the mine. Most were from Racalmuto, but there were many from other nearby towns: Montedoro, Grotte, and Serradifalco. Those from the latter town lived even further from the mine than Nino, and their cart trips took over an hour each way.

One night in June, as Nino prepared to clamber into the *carrozza* that would carry him home, one of the mine owners took him aside.

Don Morreale began, "Your son Saverio –"

Nino corrected him, "Salvatore".

"Yes, uh, right, Salvatore." Well, we need *carusi*. Two died last week. We can pay you a *succursu* for Salvatore – twenty *scuti*."

"Twenty *scuti*! For my son's life?"

"If you don't like it, you can speak to some of the *picuneri* who get their own *carusi*."

Nino had already done this, and knew that none of the pickmen would pay more than eighteen *scuti*. Further, their *carusi* had to scramble to find a place to sleep at night, while the owner's *carusi* had a separate space, even if it was only a wide place at the end of a played-out tunnel. And the scraps of stale food that the owners supplied their *carusi* were at least provided regularly. The individual pickmen were less likely to give their helpers enough food, and their personal tenure over the boys led to treatment that was often no better than a slave might receive.

Though Nino had never been able to afford his own *carusi*, he was intuitively grateful that he had never been in the position of virtually owning another person. "This practice can only scorch the souls of the *picuneri* as well those of the *carusi*." he thought.

But it was a vicious cycle. Because he could not afford to contract for *carusi*, he was paid a lower wage than those who could, so he needed the *succursu* payment. Twenty *scuti* could provide for his family's subsistence, meager as it might be, for six months. In a country with a language that had no future tense, six months was an inconceivable leap into the future. Reluctantly, Nino accepted the offer.

Morreale presented him with a note that could be exchanged in town for twenty *scuti*, and had him make his mark on two copies of a contract stipulating the terms of the agreement. "Your wife can take the note to the *municipio* tomorrow, to exchange it for money, and she can have the clerk confirm the contract."

"What does it say?"

"That the boy Salvatore Alessi will work as a *carusu* at this mine, that he will be fed, clothed and boarded here, and take orders from the *picuneri* that he is assigned to. For his services, you will receive twenty *scuti*."

Nino knew that the "*fed, clothed and boarded*" part of the contract would constitute poor provisions indeed, while the onerous orders his son must obey would be almost overwhelming. Nevertheless, he felt he had no choice, if he was to keep the rest of his family alive, so he accepted the voucher and the contract, and climbed aboard the *carrozza*.

26

That night, Maria Rizzo could not sleep, and she left the sleeping-room and quietly trod down to the living quarters. She lit a tiny fire in the hearth that doubled as a room heater and cooking-place, using only a few twigs from their diminishing bundle. She sat on a sawed-off log that served as a bench, staring into the flickering flames. In their sprightly dance, she saw Totò, a lithe, laughing miniature of the grandfather for whom he had been named, Maria's father-in-law Salvatore Alessi. Like his *nannu* Salvatore, Totò had a strong brow and square jaw, belying his youth, but also like his namesake, it seemed he was perpetually smiling, always in motion. To her son's wraith in the flames, Maria whispered "Your *nannu* died in a war that was to help us *puvureddi*, but you will die in a mine, because we are *still* poor.

Next morning, Maria Alessi rose when Nino and Totò did. They broke fast on her fresh bread and some cheese she had managed to make from the goat's dwindling supply of milk. She had made an ingenious garment for Totò, a sort of tunic that covered his shoulders and reached to his knees. It was doubled at the waist so that it could be let down to cover his legs. "See, do this if you need to stay warm." she said.

"Warmth won't be a problem in the depths of the mine," interjected Nino "Most of the time we go almost naked because of the heat."

"Well, he must go outdoors to the privy, even in winter. This will help. And see this?" Sewn inside, against Totò's body, the garment had a pouch which could be reached through a slit concealed by a fold of cloth.

"Here is a cheese and a hard sausage. Put them in the pouch, and tell no one," she said. She embraced him and went down to the cart with them. Nino lifted the tearful Totò into the cart and then climbed in. He reached out to the violently sobbing Maria. Never one to show much emotion, he put his arm around her shoulder and pressed his cheek to hers, whispering "*Mariù*, I'm sorry. I'll do my best to protect him at the mine. I'm sorry you have had to lose the first Totò, and now this one, too, our eldest son. I'm so sorry, two beautiful sons . . ."

But the cart lurched away, tearing him from her as she cried, unheard, "And a daughter, I've lost a daughter, too!"

Chapter 4.

Totò had been at the mine for a few weeks. Some *carusi* worked only for the pickmen who held their contracts, while Totò and a group of others were assigned to those men who could not afford to offer families the *succursu*, to acquire their own *carusi*. He had quickly fallen into the same routine as the other *carusi*, some who were as old as his father. He could not help but look at their thin, wizened bodies, pale from lack of sun, and their graying heads, and wonder if this was his fate. Though he was still not fully acclimated to the netherwordly stench of the sulfur, these men had had it infused into their very beings. If they ever chanced to enter a town, their odor would make their presence known before they were seen. Totò wondered why they didn't smell as bad as when he had arrived, but then with distaste he realized that it was because he, himself, was acquiring that unpleasant aura.

The mine entrance was nothing more than a wide hole in the side of a mountain. Uncounted decades ago, someone had started to chop away at some limestone that was streaked with yellow. As the vein of sulfur was followed, the hole eventually became a tunnel that snaked down along the path of the sulfur as it had been deposited in the rock. By Totò's time, the mine had numerous winding passages, some leading down into the mountain for more than a kilometer. In some places, crude steps had been carved, while other routes were without such amenities. At intervals, narrow vertical shafts had been dug from above, into the tunnels to permit limited amounts of fresh air and daylight. In spite of a few haphazardly placed timbers, in some spots, portions of the tunnel roofs had collapsed.

First thing each morning, the *carusi* ate as much food as they could from the scant provisions put out by the mine owners or their pickmen. They would snatch bites of food as they could through the day, but when night came, they would be too exhausted to eat, and cared only for sleep.

When the boys were ready, each pickman, followed by two or three *carusi*, would descend to the end of the particular tunnel he was working, and begin chopping away at the yellow vein. As the pile of sulfur-bearing rock accumulated, each *carusu* would fill a canvas bag: five kilos for the seven year-olds, graduating to about fifteen kilos for the teenagers and as much as thirty kilos for the grown men. The bearer would then prop the stiff sack on his shoulder and make his way, often a kilometer or more, up the sloping tunnel to the mouth of the mine. If a tunnel was wide enough, two pickmen might work side by side, but their piles of rock were kept separate. The *carusu* assigned to each must be sure to transport only the material excavated by his own master.

It was a tortuous path, difficult enough without any burden. With the sulfur on their backs, it was bone-wearying. The depths of the mine were so hot that all, *picuneri* and *carusi* alike, toiled virtually naked, dressed only in loincloths.

Totò was unlucky to have started his life as a ca-rusu in summer. It was so hot that they baked, not just in the mine but outside as well, in the stifling air around the smelting furnaces. The doors to the smelt-ers seemed like maws that ate their loads of sulfur as quickly as the bearers could dump them.

In winter, even dressed lightly, the interior of the mine was still barely endurable, but they froze in the outside air. They could wear rough clothing that gave some comfort outside, but it made the depths even more unbearable. Most chose to go nearly naked even in the cold season, and many who did so suffered the consequences of exposure or pneumonia. Some died.

After the sulfur was dumped, each *carusu* hurriedly retrieved his sack and rushed back into the tunnels. This was not because of dedication to their work. If the pickman had chopped more sulfur in their absence than they could load on their next trip, he would rage at them, spit at them, and berate them, for he was paid according to the amount of the mineral that his *carusi* delivered to the smelter. Many a pickman did more than curse, especially if he had his own contract for his *carusi*. They would be scuffed, kicked or pinched until they screamed. They did not tarry on their return trips.

As each day wore on, the floors and walls of the dark, tortuous tunnels would become slippery with the sweat of the ever-moving *carusi*. This might be worsened by patches of vomit or urine, where a boy had lost control. If a *carusu* on the way up had to pass another on the way down, the loaded boy had the right of way, but in tight quarters he still had to squirm past, one body bumping against the other. The odd clump of rock that might tumble from a sack made the footing even more treacherous, and in the weeks since Totò arrived, several bearers had fallen, including one who would rise no more. The dead boy's pickman merely cursed that now his production would be limited until he could find another *carusu*.

Antonino, when he could, would bring a dry sausage or a crust of bread or cheese, which he would surreptitiously pass to Totò, to be hidden in the secret pouch until needed. Occasionally, Totò would be assigned as one of his father's *carusi*, and between grunts, as he chopped at the rock, Nino would manage to convey Maria's love, and to tell the boy something of the world outside.

One day Nino was working at the end of a tunnel in an area which had been widened into a chamber which could hold several pickmen and their boys. Totò was working with him. The pickmen, when working together in this way, would fall into a rhythm, chanting nonsense syllables, each string ending with an "Ummph!" as their picks struck the rock in unison. Totò struggled to keep up with the growing pile of ore, but as he was filling his sack, he mistakenly picked up a rock from the pile belonging to the next miner, *u Bruttu*. The man's cruel face, hairy back and bulging muscles warranted the only name he was known by, "the Brute".

Seeing the boy pick up ore that belonged to him, *u Bruttu* launched a mighty swing at Totò. Luckily, the lad was nimble. He jumped to the side so that the huge hand struck a glancing blow, nevertheless driving him against the rock face, and inflicting a gash on his shoulder.

Nino sprang between his son and the attacker, shouting "Let him be!"

"Out of the way!" roared *u Bruttu*, "He's just a lousy *carusu*, I'll teach him a lesson!"

Nino, much smaller than *u Bruttu*, stood his ground. The hairy brute took a step towards him and started to speak, but just as he opened his mouth, Nino took a mighty swing, from his knees to the point of *u Bruttu's* jaw. Years of chopping sulfur had given Nino arms of steel, and the big man's jaw snapped shut, breaking several teeth, and he slumped back, unconscious.

The other miners and their *carusi* stared open-mouthed, as did Totò. Nino looked at his son's shoulder, dismissed the wound as a scratch, and said, "All right, don't stand there, fill your sack and go! And don't pick up the wrong ore!" He then turned to the others and said "See that none of you, miner or *carusu*, ever lays a hand on my son." And with that he raised his pick and resumed his relentless attack on the vein of sulfur.

That night, by the light of torches fueled by the plentiful sulfur and set in the rock walls, Totò returned to a mine chamber where niches were carved for Don Morreale's *carusi* to sleep in. He wet his hands in a communal tub of tepid water, swiped the perspiration from his face, and fell into the makeshift bunk, asleep before he felt its hard surface.

Outside the mine, like the other *picuneri*, and as ancient athletes had done, Nino scraped the sweat and soil from his naked body with a curved wooden slat, before donning his clothing. He and the other pickmen crowded into the *carrozza*, leaving Totò and the other *carusi* behind. *U Bruttu*, a coward at heart, meekly made way for him and even nudged others to provide space for "*u Martiddu*, Alessi". *U Martiddu*, "the Hammer", became Nino's nickname among his co-workers. When he arrived home, Maria, as always, asked him worriedly, "How is he? How is my son?"

And Nino, as always, answered, "*Campa ancora* - he still lives."

33

Chapter 5.

For several years, life went on without much change for Antonino Alessi's family. Each day, the cart carried Nino to his dusk-to-dawn labors at *Rumpispaddi*, where he protected his son Totò as best he could. Maria Rizzo kept the household running, within her means. She was thankful that by using the *succursu* they received for poor Totò and the few *sordi* she earned for the fine *puntina* lace she produced, they had not had to send her other son Tanuzzu to the mines. Her eldest daughter Grazia was a good little girl who not only helped when her mother sewed lace, but watched over little Giuseppa so that 'Pina' would not be under foot when Maria was cooking or cleaning.

By 1876, farming had become somewhat more fruitful, and many erstwhile pickmen had left the mines to go back to the farms, or to join the trickle of emigration to America, a drip that would become a flood by the end of the century. However temporarily, these factors had a positive effect on the wages earned by mine workers. Eleven-year old Grazia was now producing lace that rivaled her mother's in beauty and quality, and with their earnings and Nino's higher wages, the family had been able to set some money aside.

Then Nino had approached Don Morreale and told him that he and Maria had saved a sum of money. Morreale had pouted and said "I suppose now you'll get your own *carusi* and want a higher wage?" But Nino had said "No. Here's Totò's contract, and here are twenty *scuti*. I'm paying back the *succursu*, and I want my son." Thus Nino was able to free his son from the near-slavery of the *carusi*. Morreale, meanwhile, silently cursed himself for not including usurious interest in the contract. He'd never thought of it, as in his memory, no parent had ever bought one back.

Nino had ever been one of the hardest-working *picuneri*, and in 1881 he was made a crew master at the mine, with several pickmen under his supervision. One of them was his son, Salvatore 'Totò' Alessi. As a *picuneri*, Totò now also earned a wage, which he contributed wholly to the family's resources. Like his father, Totò had empathy with the *carusi*. The other pickmen, at least in the presence of the Alessi men, softened their treatment of the sulfur bearers. The pickman's work was often competitive, with men jockeying for position at the richest veins. In an environment hostile to conversation or camaraderie, Totò still managed to make friends. One was Leonardo '*Narduzzu*' Coniglio, from Serradifalco.

One day at the mine, Narduzzu tripped while chopping at a stubborn outcrop and severely scraped his right arm, which bled profusely. The usual procedure was for the owners to ignore any injury, and to begin planning for a new *picuneri*.

The other pickmen were too concerned with chopping ore to be bothered with their fellows' problems. But Totò, seeing Coniglio's heavily bleeding arm, pulled out the rope that was securing his loincloth, and naked, used it for a crude tourniquet to stanch the flow. Totò's action may have saved Coniglio's life, his arm, and his job, or it may not have been necessary. Regardless, Narduzzu became his unflinching friend. Using his town's diminutive for the name Salvatore, he called Totò "my *cumpari, Turiddu*."

The bond between them blossomed into a friendship among their families, and on the occasional Sunday, the entire Alessi clan would journey on the new *ferrovia*, the railroad from Racalmuto to Serradifalco, to help Narduzzu's family celebrate a feast day. Alternately, sometimes the Coniglios would trek to Racalmuto.

Totò's sister Grazia had married and become part of her husband's household. Pina now helped in the lace-making that augmented the family's income. Tanuzzu had been spared working as a *carusu* and was a happy, healthy teen-ager whose intelligence had landed him a job, helping at the pharmacy of the mayor. If he could learn the duties of a clerk he might escape the heavy labor of the *picuneri*.

The family's life was by no means luxurious, but, after the first Salvatore's death, and the 'miscarriage', the other children had survived and there had usually been enough for them to eat. Thankfully, Maria and Nino had produced no more children. For Maria Rizzo, however, no amount of good fortune could ease the pain she still harbored in her heart, after giving up her beautiful green-eyed girl. But shame, and worry that her husband would be devastated, kept her from revealing her secret.

At the foundling home of the *Chiesa Madre Annunziata*, life went on as before. Foundlings, though not as many as previously, were still occasionally plucked from the wheel by Anna di Marco, ever jovial but now severely limited in her duties by her arthritic bones. She and Padre Raimondo still chose names for the infants, and found wet-nurses. Now and again, foundlings would be taken at a very young age by mothers who had lost their own children in childbirth or accidents, and who had milk to nourish the abandoned babies.

Half the infants who remained in Anna's care died within a year, of malnutrition, cholera, dysentery or some other disease, sometimes transmitted by the very wet-nurses who fed them. Anna cared as best she could for those who survived, in the small spaces allotted within the church grounds.

The older foundlings might be taken by *contadini* or tradesmen, as assistants in their work or as servants at their homes.

When the boys were seven, the sulfur mine owners would offer the *succursu* to the Padre, and a number of boys would be consigned as *carusi*. This led to much disagreement between Anna and Padre Raimondo. She had worked at the church before he had been ordained, and had known him as a child: "*Ramú*" she would say, "How can you send these children to such a fate?"

But the priest had little choice. If he was to provide for the foundlings who remained, he had to take every "donation" that was offered. It was endemic in Sicily that some must suffer much, to allow others to simply survive. While Padre Raimondo succumbed to this cruel arrangement, unlike pastors in other towns, he refused to sell the *Chiesa Annunziata's* girl foundlings into lives of prostitution.

Sometimes a woman, married or not, would go to the *municipio* and ask to see the record of births for a certain day in a certain year. She could then determine the name that had been given to the uniquely-dressed child she had left in the wheel, and claim it as her own. In the same way, couples, too, might seek out a child they had once been unable to support. Anna had never found a dependable wet-nurse for Rosa Esposto in the town, so the green-eyed girl had been passed from one to another in the foundling home. They gave her little besides their milk, and it was Anna who changed and bathed and dressed her. Until she grew too tall, Anna laid her to sleep in the basket beside her own bed. In twelve years, no one had come to claim the 'child of the red slippers'.

Rosa Esposto had become Anna di Marco's 'helping angel'. Ever since she had been a small child, Rosa was curious about the babes that Anna took from the wheel, and as soon as she had grown enough to do so, she would help with their care. Now almost thirteen, she was growing into a lovely young woman who took joy in caring for them when old Anna was limited by her infirmities.

Whenever she saw him reading the church's beautiful vellum bible, Rosa pestered Padre Raimondo so much that he relented and taught her to read. He would even reluctantly lend her books from his modest library. She had also learned Anna's arts as a spinner, weaver and seamstress. She used them well, to repair the foundlings' clothes, and her own. Sometimes a kindly merchant would donate tailings from a bolt of cloth. Rosa would work wonders with it. She would try to let every child benefit, even if it meant only a new bandana or a bright new patch in a pair of worn trousers. Occasionally, she even managed to create a handkerchief or shawl for herself.

She began a custom of handing out the modest presents once a month, before Sunday Mass. Her heart would swell when the ragged little ones would scramble about her ankles, laughing and crying out for the gifts, shouting "Mamma Rosa, Mamma Rosa!"

Rosa was friends with Alba di Giugno and Santa Proietto, and some of the other girls on the grounds. Alba and Santa were two lively teenagers who shared Rosa's cramped cubicle at night and worked as servants for townspeople during the day. She preferred their company to that of the wet-nurses, some of whom had unsavory pasts, which in fact had resulted in pregnancies that then led them to serve in the home. One had brought with her a baby born out of wedlock, and alternated between nursing her own infant and a foundling.

There were boys as well, at the makeshift church orphanage, but they were segregated and usually saw the girls at a distance during Mass, and at noonday meals in the church scullery. Rosa did know a boy who was a 'friend', if one with whom she had exchanged a few pleasantries could be called that: he was not a foundling, but Pietro Castiglione, the youngest son of Racalmuto's *sindaco*, or mayor.

Mass was sung every morning at the *Chiesa Annunziata*, and for some time, tall, blond Pietro had been an altar boy. One of his fellow acolytes, and a good friend, was short, dark Tanuzzu Alessi, who, unbeknownst to Rosa, was her brother.

At times, when the girls from one side of the church were filing back to their duties, and the altar boys just happened to be standing in the aisle as they passed, Pietro's grey eyes would meet Rosa's green gems. He would mumble "*'iurnu, signurina Esposto*," and her red cheeks would grow ever redder, as she would flutter her lowered black lashes and respond "*'iurnu* – good day."

Chapter 6.

Because of its southern location and the moderating waters that surround it, Sicily, the gem of the Mediterranean, has mild winters, and pleasant springs and autumns. Summer, however, is a beast of a different stripe. In July and August, the island is subjected to the hot south wind, the *scirocco*, that sweeps up from Africa and sometimes seems to scorch the very stones of Sicily.

On one such hot summer evening, the cramped dormitories of the foundling home were so stifling that the children could not get to sleep. Hearing sighs, sobs and moans from the restless children, Anna Di Marco fretted so in their shared cubicle that Rosa arose and said, "Try to rest, Signura Anna, I'll see if I can do something to relieve the little ones."

Rosa roused them all out to the stone courtyard of the church. In daytime, the area was shaded from the glaring Sicilian sun, and at night its pavement was somewhat cooler than the surroundings. The children felt some relief, though in the hot breeze it seemed they caught the faint scent of African sand and spices.

As they sat cross-legged around their mentor, the children clamored "Mama Rosa, Mama Rosa, tell us a story, *pir favuri*," and Rosa responded "All right, I'll tell you a fable, to keep you cool!"

This is the tale she told:

"Many years ago, there was a poor couple, Gino and Gina. They were *contadini*, sharecroppers who tilled the land of a *patruni*, but could keep only a small portion of the fruits of their labors to feed themselves.

"They had to give the lion's share of the crops to their landlord. They lived in a tiny wooden hut near a small town right here in Sicily.

"The name of the town was *Ciumifriddu,* which as you know means 'cold river', and the hut was on the banks of that chilly river.

"One night, Gina lamented to Gino, 'Here we live in this miserable hut, sleeping on straw on this dirt floor, like animals. If we had a decent bed, *'nu littu,* I could at least sleep comfortably after the day's labor.' (Some of the children sighed dreamily, wishing that they, too, might someday have a real bed.)

"Gino scoffed, 'And where would we get a bed? We haven't a *rinali pir pisciari* (at this, the foundlings giggled), nor a stool to sit on.'

"Gina retorted '*Nu maritu affittuosu* (a loving husband) would find a way to get us a bed.'

"Thereafter, Gina couldn't repress her wish for a bed. Every day, she would hound Gino ~ 'a bed, a bed!' ~ morning, noon and night.

"Finally, Gino could take no more. One day when Gina was working the far side of the fields, he began to strip boards from one side of the hut. He took them out back to a dark *motta,* a grove of trees, where he began sawing and pounding.

"That night, Gina had new complaints. 'You're not doing your fair share of the hoeing and planting. I finished twice as many rows as you did today! I'm exhausted, and not only must I sleep on straw, now there's a *pirtusu,* a hole in the wall, and the wind from that

42

cold river freezes my *coscie!*'" (The children breathed deeply, as if to inhale the refreshing coolness.)

Rosa continued: "It went on that way for a week. The hole got bigger and bigger, the cold wind blew with more force, and Gina's complaints grew shriller.

"She was so angry with Gino that she would work in the fields as far away from him as she could. Gino seemed to be wasting away with concern. Then, one late afternoon while Gina was trudging back towards the hut, Gino intercepted her and said 'Come with me to the grove ~ I have a surprise.'

"When they entered the grove, Gina couldn't believe her eyes. There beneath the trees was a magnificent four-poster bed, hung with satins and holding a huge feather mattress. Gina was overcome with joy, and she embraced Gino as they fell into the warm softness of the bed, and, ahem, did what adults do in bed." (The youngest children adopted quizzical looks, while the older ones smirked knowingly.)

"Next morning, Gina asked 'But where did you get these fine bed-linens?' and Gino replied 'I have sold my share of our food every night, to pay *Donna Chidda* for the linens.'

"Gina stroked the dark, polished wood of the bed, and began to ask 'And the wood . . . ?' but just then she looked out of the grove, toward the cold river, and cried 'Our hut – it's gone! What happened to our hut?'

"Gino shrugged and with a sheepish smile, he answered: '*La froscia 'unn si fa senza rumpiri l'ova.* You can't make an omelet without breaking the eggs!'"

Just as Rosa finished her story, the courtyard

echoed with the sound of the chimes of the foundling wheel. Alerted, Rosa shooed the now-sleepy children "Quickly, quickly, all of you! Up to your dormitories and to sleep! I must tend to the wheel, and see what new playmate it has brought you!

Chapter 7.

By the summer of 1883, Maria Rizzo could wait no longer. She had to know what had become of her daughter. Had she survived, or, like so many others, had she died of cholera and been buried in the church-yard? Was she one of the girls who worked for the gentry of the town? Was she the one with dark curls who sat with the other foundling girls at Mass? Maria had never been able to get close enough to see the girl's eyes, but then, it seemed as though every young girl reminded her of her baby. She would have been nearly fifteen by now, almost a grown woman.

As the handsome son of the mayor, young Pietro Castiglione was known to most townspeople. Pietro had a happy disposition, and though his family was privi-leged, he was a friend to boys of all classes, and was not above doing chores for any of the village residents. In spite of his height, they called him *Pitruzzu*, little rock. One scorching July day, as he was passing Via Spina, he saw his friend Tanuzzu's mother, Maria Rizzo. She was struggling to steady a large jug of water on her head with one hand, while with the other she led her goat from the small patch of grass near the town fountain. The uneven cobblestone street made the balancing act even harder.

"*Signura, lassassi fari a mia!* Ma'am, let me do that for you!" Pietro took the jug and carried it across the street and up to the Alessi family's living quarters, while Maria secured the goat on the ground floor. When he came down she thanked him for his kindness, and then had a thought.

"Pitruzzu, at your father's office, at the *municipio* -

the town's ledgers, they are free for all to see, no?"

"Yes", he replied, "they're available when someone needs to check a record, if they want to marry, or buy property and such."

"It is not seemly for a woman to go alone through the streets to the office. My husband and my son Totò are away at the mine all day. Tanuzzu works at your father's shop and doesn't have time to accompany me. Could you look at the ledgers for me?"

"*Certu, signura.* What would you like me to search for?"

"On a day in early January, in 1869, a child was found on the wheel. She was wearing a white silk hat and red slippers. Do you think you could tell me what name she was given?"

Pietro raised an eyebrow, but looked away so that Maria did not see. She didn't say why she wanted the information, and he didn't ask.

"I'll talk to Pepe, the scribe, and ask to see the ledger. *'arrivederci, signura.*"

"*Grazie"* Maria whispered, her heart in her mouth.

Pietro set off to Via Vittorio Emanuele and the town offices, which had taken over an old monastery building. He waved to the men lounging outside, including messers Avenia and Puma, still chewing cheroots and discussing politics. In the office, Giuseppe Arnone, the scribe, was bent over a parchment, his ink-stained hands carefully transcribing a record. He said to himself "Now, here's the boss's son, I hope he's not here to spy on me." But Pietro's good nature kept Pepe from being too concerned.

"*Misca!*" said Pietro. "All these huge books! There must be hundreds of records!"

"Thousands. In 1815, Napoleon ordered all Europe to keep uniform records. Though they threw Napoleon's nephew out of Spain, our previous rulers the Spanish Bourbons admired the system, and since 1820, our town has complied with it. Our records are even better and more complete than those of the *norte'taliani*. I, myself have worked here going onto forty years, and during that time, have personally recorded the birth, marriage, and death of every single *paisanu!*"

"I'll bet you don't have <u>every</u> year." said Pietro in a mocking tone.

Arnone stiffened. "I certainly do!"

"<u>Any</u> year?"

"After 1820, yes!"

"Let's see them! How about 1867, the year *I* was born?"

"You impudent boy, it just happens that I have the ledger right here. I was making a note on the birth record of Antonia Liotta, that she has married Vincenzo Scime. His wife died and he took himself another, younger one, to care for his six children." Pepe turned the ledger towards Pietro and said "Here, look for yourself."

Pietro gingerly took the huge volume and surreptitiously leafed past 1867, to the records for 1869. "Early

January," *signura* Maria had said. Then, there under record number 9, he saw the words "today, January 7, 1869, Anna di Marco, age 65, Ruotaia, presented a baby girl found on the public wheel. The child has black curls and green eyes, and is dressed in a white silk cap . . . and red slippers." Pietro gulped and continued to read: ". . . the parents being unknown, the name given to the child is *Rosa*, and the surname given to her is *Esposto*."

Pietro's face paled and then flushed, as he gently closed the ledger and carefully handed it back to the scribe.

Anna di Marco was gravely ill.

Over eighty years old, she had picked up a sickness borne to her by one of her children of the wheel; but unlike the infant, she had not been able to shake it. Rosa hovered over the old woman, the closest thing to a mother that she had known, and tried to comfort her. Finally, deep in the night, Anna's fever had burned so, and her cries echoed so pitifully, that Rosa ran to waken the priest. By the time they returned, Anna was still moaning, but her fever had turned to chills, even in the hot July night.

Padre Raimondo had been hardened by the deaths of countless numbers of his faithful, but Anna had served him and their charges long and well, and he could barely choke back a sob as he said, "I'm sorry, child, but it's best that I give her the Last Rites."

Raimondo prepared the trappings and unguents of the ceremony, and said the requisite prayers over Anna's body, a shell of the robust woman she had been. He finished just as she uttered one final gasp.

As the last breath of life escaped Anna's lips, Rosa and the priest heard a loud jangling. "The chimes," Rosa cried, "the wheel!"

Later that morning, at the *municipio*, mayor Castiglione and Pepe Arnone recorded the death of Anna di Marco and the birth of a new foundling boy, to whom had been given the name *Giovanni* and the surname *Trovato*.

Pepe looked up from his chore, to the black-haired, green-eyed woman-child who had presented the infant, and asked "What shall I put down as your occupation?

With a bewildered look, Rosa Esposto exclaimed: *"Ruotaia."*

Chapter 8.

That Saturday following the morning Mass, Padre Raimondo directed two of his altar boys, Pietro Castiglione and his friend Tanuzzu Alessi, to fetch water from the town fountain for the new *ruotaia*, and to help her scrub floors in the dormitory rooms. Pietro went gladly, with Tanuzzu grumbling alongside. On their way back from the well, each burdened by a yoke holding two brim-full wooden buckets of water, Tanuzzu complained "Why did Padre give *us* this chore? He could have picked Carmelo or Vincenzo."

"Ah, *Panzariddu*," Pietro replied, using Tanuzzu's nickname, 'little belly.' "I don't mind. Rosa works hard taking care of the *trovatelli*, the little foundlings."

"Rosa, Rosa, Rosa! That's all you think or talk of. I'd imagine that you, the son of the mayor, would have more important things on your mind." Tanuzzu dreamed of attending seminary and one day replacing Padre Raimondo. Far-fetched as the idea was, it made him tend to be preachy. He was above being concerned with mere girls.

"Hahaha! I may be the mayor's son, but I *am* his *son*, and not his daughter, and so why shouldn't I like girls?"

"But *that* one? She's so haughty, she acts like a queen, not the *miscina* bastard that she really is!"

Now just outside the foundlings' door, Pietro slowly lowered his buckets and turned icily towards Tanuzzu. "You shouldn't say things about people if you don't know they're true!"

"Allright, allright, don't get angry. Let's finish this so we can go hunting rabbits."

While Tanuzzu tended the fire that heated the water in a huge cauldron, Pietro and Rosa swept the floors and then scoured them with hot water and bristle brushes, working side by side. Pietro asked: "Rosa, you are the *ruotaia* now. Can you leave the grounds?"

"You ask me such questions, and you know my name, but I don't even know yours!" she retorted.

"But you do so, although you've never called me by name. I'm Pietro Castiglione. You can call me Pitruzzu.

"Well, I can go outside when the market sets up in the *piazza* by the church, every Wednesday, as long as there are two other women with me." She emphasized the word *women*. "And sometimes, with others, I take some children for walks in the fields, near the grove of almonds."

"You like caring for the children?"

"They're my responsibility. They get little enough love or care. I try to show them that they're important. And I love to see them smile, or even laugh when I can give them some little gift like a new cap that I've sewn."

"Do you ever dream of leaving this, of living in a real house, or of getting married?"

"Married? Hah! Who would pay my dowry? And who would marry a foundling, without even a name of her own?"

"What if you *had* a name?"

52

"And what if I had a horse, and a carriage, and a palace? Why dream of just a name when I can dream of all that? Anyway . . ."

Just then, Rosa's foot slipped on a wet cobble, and she lost her balance. Pietro dropped his brush and grasped her by the waist, righting her. But even after she regained her feet, he held tight. They were face to face, with one of his arms around her waist. Her green eyes looked into his, and her rosy cheeks darkened. She broke away, and Pietro stuttered, "Well even without a name, *someone* might want to marry you!"

Rosa regained her composure and laughed "Allright, we're done with the floors and I have children to take care of. You and your friend had better leave."

As they left, Rosa recalled the boys' conversation, which she had heard when they were outside her door. "Pietro defended me," she thought, "He is my *Petru*, my rock."

Tanuzzo and Pietro had agreed that Pietro would call for his stubby friend after the noon meal. As he approached the Alessi house, he saw *signura* Rizzo on her balcony, hanging recently-washed laundry. She called down: "Tanuzzu is out gathering kindling. He'll be right back. Wait there."

She met him at the stoop, a little out of breath. Though she wore a shawl, he noticed for the first time that graying, once-black curls framed her face. And he noticed that her eyes were green. Maria hesitated, then blurted: "Did you see the register?"

"*Si, signura,*" he answered "the baby with the red slippers was given the name Rosa Esposto. She's the new *ruotaia.*

Chapter 9.

Pietro and Tanuzzu stalked through high grass towards an old oak with gnarled roots protecting a rabbit warren. Tanuzzu held a *pistola* and Pietro cradled a *lupara* shotgun in the crook of his right arm.

The guns were the boys' fathers. Even though Pietro was the younger, he had his father's permission to use his firearms, and could have chosen any of them. But Tanuzzu had removed the *pistola* from the secret place in which he had seen his father Antonino hide it. There would be hell to pay if his father discovered that he was using it.

They crept closer to the barrow, and suddenly a rabbit that had been frozen in position darted for cover. Tanuzzu could only watch open-mouthed, while Pietro stood, shouldered the *lupara* and pulled the trigger. Then, several things happened at once. The gun emitted a mighty flash and a roar, the rabbit flew into his hole, and Pietro was knocked backward, next to Tanuzzu, onto his rump.

The young men looked at each other in surprise, then both broke into laughter so hard that it brought tears. In the many times they had gone "hunting", this was the first time either of them had got off a shot. They laughed until they ached, then brushed themselves off and headed back home.

"That was wonderful," cried Tanuzzu: "you actually *shot* at it! We've never had such luck!"

The traveling market came to the Via Garibaldi neighborhood every Wednesday. Vendors set up makeshift stalls, from which they cried out in sing-song, offering fresh fruit, bread, milk and meat, as well as various drygoods for the townspeople's appraisal. Maria Rizzo went every week, not for bread, which she made herself, nor milk, which her goat supplied, but for the fruit, olives and greens the vendors displayed, and, rarely, for a morsel of ham or beef.

The family was building a nest egg from savings put aside from the wages Nino and Totò earned at the mine, along with Tanuzzu's contribution. Proceeds from the occasional sale of lace, painstakingly handmade by Pina and herself, added to the fund. Maria prayed that it would one day enable them to buy a little *campagna*, a small plot of land on the outskirts of town that would allow them to grow their own vegetables, and possibly oranges and even olives. For now, however, she had to haggle with the vendors if she wanted such luxuries as fruit or olives.

But today her mind was not on shopping. As she looked distractedly at the vendors' wares, a corner of her eye concentrated on the side door of the *Chiesa Annunziata*, the door to the orphan's quarters. "Are you going to buy something, or just poke and squeeze my produce?" asked a gnarled, sunburned *contadino*. "Eh, if I happen to see anything that won't poison me, I may buy it!" she retorted, then caught her breath as she saw several figures leaving the orphanage. Rosa Esposto was among them.

While Rosa's companions excitedly looked over the dresses at one vendor's stall, the practical *ruotaia* headed for the foodstuffs to see whether she could find any bargains. A woman she recognized, Tanuzzu's mother Maria Rizzo, gestured to her, and they both stepped toward a stone bench a little apart from the patrons crowding the stalls. "*S - signurina*," Maria said haltingly, "I - I wish to tell you something."

After Maria had revealed her secret, Rosa stood dumbly, for a moment unable to speak or even breathe. Hesitantly, Maria said: "Please don't hate me. I . . ."

"Hate you? I love you! You don't know how I have longed for a mother, for someone to claim me. Oh, mamma!" Rosa embraced Maria and together they fell back onto the bench, sobbing and kissing each other's cheeks.

Chapter 10.

As *ruotaia*, Rosa had the advantage over her late mentor Anna Di Marco, in that her youth made it easier to keep up with the younger charges, playing games with them and taking them for walks, as Anna had been unable to do in her waning years. But nothing could ease her near panic, each time in the middle of the night when she would hear the bells that announced the arrival of another abandoned infant. And her youth did not lessen the pain she felt when she saw the hardships imposed on the foundlings.

It started with their naming.

Earlier, in the 1500's, the use of surnames, or family names, was not widespread. Nobility were identified by their first, or Christian given names, and by the name of the town, or castle, or mountain, that they commanded. Serfs and peasants generally lived in such small communities that a simple given name would suffice each. But first names might not be enough. If, for example, there were three men named Giovanni in a village, one might be called according to his trade, Giovanni *il fornaro* (John the baker), another by his father's name, Giovanni *figlio di Tommaso* (John, son of Thomas), and another by a physical trait: Giovanni lo curto (John the short). Eventually, as feudal lords required more strict accounts of their subjects, for tax purposes and to impose military service, they made laws which required everyone to have a surname. So one Giovanni was Giovanni Fornaro, the second was Giovanni Di Tommaso, and the other was called Giovanni Lo Curto.

Surnames derived in this way were often the rule.

And in small cities like Racalmuto, the limited population also meant that there were relatively few surnames to go around, to the extent that a Sicilian's home town could often be determined simply by knowing that his surname was common in this village or that.

When civil records of births first began to be kept in the early 1800's, if the child was a foundling, no surname at all was imposed, reverting back to a single given name. The child was then known as "Teresa *la trovatella*" (Teresa the foundling), or "Luigi *proiettu*" (cast-off Louis) and so on. By the time Rosa was found in the wheel, these descriptions had become the equivalent of surnames, thus she was named Rosa Esposto (Rosa, exposed to the elements). Foundlings were stigmatized by their surnames even if they somehow found lives outside of the foundling homes. Later, the practice was modified, but not very charitably.

Instead of surnames literally or figuratively meaning 'foundling', these children were given names that were 'different'. An abandoned child might be named Giuseppe Verdi ~ a fine Italian name, namesake of the great composer, but if the town was Racalmuto, and there were no families in town with the surname Verdi, everyone villager knew that *their* Giuseppe Verdi was a foundling, an orphan, or worse, a bastard. The same held true for surnames like Gelsomino (Jasmine) and Giumento (Jackass), or names derived from distant places, like Messina, Palermo, or Siragusa.

Eventually, when men with such names married, their children took the same surname, and through familiarity, many of the 'foundling names' became less and less of a stigma. However, some, whether they were thought by a parish priest to be humorous, or were given with malice, never ceased to be humiliating for their bearers. One such case was that of Angela the foundling.

Angela was brought to the wheel almost four years after Rosa had been deposited there. One of Rosa's earliest recollections was the night the old *ruotaia* Anna Di Marco had brought a filthy, squealing bundle up to the cubicle they shared. Rosa only vaguely remembered that event, and hearing Anna exclaim "The *puvira picciridda* must have been born in a coal pile!"

Since Rosa herself had become *ruotaia*, she had made it a point to visit the *municipio* often, to review the birth records of the babes who had come before she was in charge, to learn what she could about their origins. Of course, it didn't hurt that in doing so, she might have a brief chance to speak to Petru Castiglione.

Old Padre Calogero, the priest who had been in charge at Rosa's christening, had still been there in 1873, when Anna Di Marco presented him with the grimy, wailing baby.

Padre Calogero was a saintly man, but tolerance of other races was not among his virtues. He had read about how the *Mauri*, the Moors or Saracens, had given Racalmuto its name, meaning 'ruined city', and he erroneously believed that they themselves had ruined the town, when in fact, they had rebuilt it. The priest just as mistakenly believed that the dark-skinned but Caucasian desert tribesmen were Negroes, for whom he used the un-saintly and unkind pejorative *milingiani*, or 'eggplants'.

Padre Calogero must have been in a foul mood when the grubby little foundling was to be named. For when Rosa Esposto, herself a child of the wheel, reviewed the

1873 birth record of that unfortunate baby, she found the usual description of its ragged swaddling clothes, and then a notation that its skin was so dirty it looked purplish-black. The child's Christian name was recorded as Angela, appropriate for the cherub-faced girl she now knew. But cruelly, the surname given to the infant was Miligiana! She was Angela the Eggplant!

Of course, the grime was soon washed away, showing little Angela to have skin that glowed like milky alabaster. But the damage was done. In those days in Sicily, even if a woman married, she kept her birth name. She would be Angela Milingiana until the day she died.

Considering Angela's situation, even when Rosa was very young, she had felt sadness, as well as a kinship with the little girl. And just as Rosa had grown to be Anna Di Marco's assistant, after Anna died, Angela had in turn become Rosa's helper. Now that Rosa knew her own identity, she felt even more sorrow over the fact that Angela might never know hers.

In spite of, or more likely because of, these sad bonds, Rosa and Angela became like sisters, and usually whenever the foundling bells chimed, both of them quickly appeared at the wheel to minister to its tiny occupant.

And chime the bells did! During Rosa's first three years as orphan-mistress, no fewer than ninety-five tiny souls had been left in the wheel, and more than half of them had perished, Even so, the small quarters the church had allotted to the foundlings was severely overcrowded.

Not all of Rosa's charges had arrived via the wheel.

Several times, relatives had personally brought in children that had been orphaned by some disaster. One tragic case involved the sulfur mine *Rumpispaddi*. A cave-in had occurred at the mine, and one poor woman had received the news that her father, her brother and her husband had all been killed. She was left with three nursing children. The tragedy had caused her breasts to wither, and she couldn't feed them. Worse, she had fallen into a deep depression, and could care for neither the children nor herself. Her sister had taken in one of the babies, a boy, but could not keep the two girls, who she had brought to the foundling home.

So many new residents were being admitted, with no decrease in sight, that the diocesan office in Girgenti finally allotted funds for a true foundling hospital to be built, attached to the church.

Chapter 11.

In those same three years, after she had finally learned of their relationship, Rosa had come to know Maria and the rest of her family. Rosa still served as the *ruotaia*, but she now slept at home, in the space vacated by Gaetano (no more 'Tanuzzu', for the priest-in-training).

After two years of sleeping in old Anna's cubicle and expertly managing the foundling home, Rosa had gained confidence in Angela Milingiana, and she had received Padre Raimondo's permission to have the girl run to inform her whenever the foundling bells rang. Rosa was at the Church every morning for Mass, and afterwards remained with the children. When they took their siesta in the early afternoon, she would walk home to have *pranzo* with her mother and sister, and then return. At sunset, leaving her charges in the care of Angela or one of the other older girls, Rosa would go back to the Alessi home and help her mother and Pina with household tasks before going to sleep.

When Nino had learned that he had a 'new' daughter, far from being saddened by her long absence or embarrassed by her status as a *proietta*, he was overwhelmed with joy and pride over her beauty, intelligence and resourcefulness.

The very next day, he went to the Mayor's office to file a *rettificazione*, a correction form, in which he declared that the baby left in the wheel in 1869 was the natural born child of himself and Maria Rizzo, his legitimate wife, and that the girl's name was officially Rosa Alessi. He also had Pepe the scribe dig out the original register of births for 1869, and had him place a margin note next to Rosa's birth record, naming himself and Maria as her parents, and giving Rosa's surname as Alessi.

Correcting Rosa's records came at no mean cost to Nino, who, to be able to visit the office to set the record straight, had to forego the cart ride to the mine. He then walked the five miles to the mine, where he was berated by Don Morreale and had his per-kilo stipend reduced by half for the remainder of the day.

The family now had its own *campagna*. With the cache that had been accumulating for years, Nino had been able to acquire a small but fruitful strip of land. It had been purchased from a couple who had sold it to raise steamship fare, to join the increasing wave of emigration to America.

The little farm was only a half-hour's walk away, and had bearing olive trees, planted by the previous owner. To them Nino had added rows of fava beans, artichokes and herbs. After Sunday Mass, Nino, Totò, Maria and Rosa would walk to the *campagna* to tend its simple treasures. Often Grazia would come with her husband and two little ones, and occasionally Gaetano was there as well, when he was home briefly from his seminary studies.

Antonino and Maria felt the irony of Gaetano's situation. As a son, he should have spared them the necessity of the dowry a family must provide when a daughter was to be wed. But during those times in Sicily, the clergy was made up primarily of sons of noble or wealthy families. The first-born sons of such families inherited the family title or its fortune, while younger sons traditionally were welcomed into the military or the priesthood. However in order for the sons of common folk to be accepted at seminary, a fee had to be paid to the institution. Nino and Maria made a show of good-natured grumbling, but for years Tanuzzu had contributed to the family everything he had earned at the pharmacy, and that contribution was one reason for their change of fortune. They gave him his "seminary dowry" with their blessing.

Pina was to be married that fall, to Giuseppe Coniglio, a sulfur miner and the son of a sulfur miner. The marriage had been arranged by Nino Alessi and Giuseppe's father, Calogero Coniglio, on one of the Alessi family's trips to Serradifalco. Calogero and his son were from that village, and both also worked at *Rumpispaddi*. They were relatives of Totò's friend Narduzzu. Pina would live in Serradifalco after her marriage, and her dowry was a chest full of beautiful hand-made lace and linens, created by herself, her mother and Rosa: enough for her own use, as well as a large surplus that the new couple could sell as they needed.

Nino, shared his family's joy in finding that he had another beautiful daughter. He was thankful that Rosa had become a contributor to the family's well-being and that she had added so much to Pina's dowry, but he was somewhat awed by her beauty and intelligence. With her addition to the family also came the knowledge that one day he would have to provide *her* dowry.

As the first week of August passed, in addition to their other *arti donnesche*, or womanly arts, the women were cooking and preparing food for the town's big *festa*. Whenever they finished their duties before Nino and Totò came back from the mine they would sit and talk, inside by candlelight in winter, and now, in summer, outdoors in the golden Sicilian twilight. Maria told family stories, and tales about Rosa's grandfathers' service with Garibaldi. In turn, Rosa recounted to her mother and sister the colorful sagas she had read in the books from the Padre's library. They were impressed and proud that Rosa could read, and marveled at the way she made wondrous fables come alive.

Three years had also been time enough for the friendship between Rosa and Pietro to develop into a budding romance. Now that Rosa spent time at the Alessi's, Pietro's friendship with Tanuzzu had given him cause to visit often.

Though there were always other family members present, the two managed, in normal conversation and friendly banter, to convey their attraction to one another. She called him *Petru*, and he called her *Rosina*. The Alessis were pleased that the son of the mayor was so friendly to their family, but mayor Castiglione felt otherwise.

"Must you spend so much time with the *puvureddi*, the poor ones?" he grumbled, "And don't get any ideas about that *ruotaia*, that nameless orphan, pretty though she may be."

"It's not their fault that they're poor. And they're not so poor that they couldn't buy a *campagna*, or give Pina an ample dowry. You know Tanuzzu was bright and a hard worker, and now he's at seminary, becoming a priest. They're good people. Furthermore, Rosa's not an orphan, nor nameless. She goes by the name Rosa Alessi. She knows who her parents are

"Hmmph! So *she* says. And don't talk back!"

But Pietro couldn't stop himself from stuttering,

despite his father's glare: "It's official. It's in the town's register of births."

Sicilians revere *San Giuseppe*, the carpenter foster-father of Christ, and to this day a number of Sicilian towns hold a *festa* to celebrate his feast day. However, St. Joseph's Day, on the calendar, is March 19; a cold, rainy, and often dreary time. But Sicilians are a practical people. So the *Racalmutesi* do the reasonable thing. They celebrate the good saint's day in August, when the weather is hot, the pigs are fat, and the trees are full of fruit. And, while March 19th occurs during Lent, when the Church forbids eating meat, in August there are no such restrictions. That was another advantage of moving the date, as far as the food-loving Sicilians were concerned. So an August feast was a feast, indeed.

Years before, the town fathers had decided to hold *San Giuseppe's* feast on the second Sunday of August. It had been that way for centuries, and the tradition continued in the summer of 1886.

During feast times, the town fathers and its citizens were less attentive to the customs that called for frugality, stoicism, and the strict separation of the sexes. People ate, drank, and were merry, and the whole town took part in the festival. So it was that in the long shadows, after a happy day of laughter and song, their feelings aroused by the communal joy around them, Rosina and Petru found a dusky, quiet grove, away from the crowd, and consummated their love.

Chapter 12.

"Chi pazzu!" "What a fool!" the mayor bellowed, "Didn't I warn you to stay away from her? Now you've disgraced us all! Your mother hasn't left her room since she heard. What a shame, *chi virgogna!*"

Pietro stood with his shoulders slumped and his head bowed. It was October, and Rosa had told him three days ago that she was sure she was with child.

"What will we do, what can we do?" his father moaned. "I spend my life achieving my position and my fool of a son makes us laughingstocks!"

"We're not laughingstocks, no one knows but the families." Pietro said defensively. "I'll marry Rosa. Many children are born early. No one needs to know."

"Marry her? The son of the mayor, marry a common *ruotaia*, a sulfur-miner's daughter? You *are* a fool. That would be more of a disgrace than what you've already done. You must leave this town. I'll write my cousin in Agrigento. You can work in his accounting office."

"No, father. I don't care what you say or do to me, I won't run away. I'm staying here."

"Well if you stay, you had better carry a weapon."

"Why?"

"Imbecile, do you know so little of honor? She has a father and two brothers. They have been shamed as well. It's their duty to avenge this disgrace. Stay if you must, but take a *pistola* and keep it with you, *loaded.*"

When his wife told him what Rosa had confided to her, Nino Alessi's reaction was no less violent than the mayor's had been. He confronted Rosa, berating her as a strumpet and a *buttana*. "And did you think you could rise above your station? That a sulfur miner wasn't good enough for you, though it was, for your sisters?" But ambivalently, he raged about Pietro's having deflowered his beautiful child.

"We must avenge this," he told her "but if I harm the son of the mayor, he will have my hide. He is a friend of Don Morreale, and he could have me fired from the mine. Neither can Totò do it, and that ... that *vigliaccu*, your cowardly brother 'Gaetano' the priest, wouldn't do anything even if I ordered him to." Nino paused and looked slyly at Rosa. "You are the wronged one, no one would hold it against you if you took revenge."

"I? But I can't hurt Petru, I love him! He loves me!"

"*Silenziu*! If he loves you so much, let him marry you. You will learn to fire a *pistola*. You will speak to Pietro. He can agree to marry you, or you will erase this dishonor."

For a month, every Sunday, Nino would walk with Rosa to the *campagna*, where he would put the pistol into her small hands and show her how to raise it in front of her, aim at a dead tree-trunk, and fire. She wept and shook at first, but eventually hardened herself to the fact that she must either do this, or be reviled by her family. She learned to hit the target.

She carried the pistol with her constantly, in a pocket of her apron. One afternoon, she was walking from the orphanage towards the Alessi home. Just as she rounded a corner, Petru stepped from the doorway of his father's shop. She confronted him in the street,

72

drew the pistol, and cried: "Marry me, or I'll kill you!"

Petru was literally petrified. He panicked, drew his own pistol and fired at Rosa: the shot was so close, it grazed her right ear. Undaunted, and with better aim, Rosa put two slugs in Petru's stomach. By the time the town marshals had arrived, the two lovers were lying in the street, but the guns had disappeared. They took a calm Rosa and an unconscious Pietro to the jailhouse.

They questioned Rosa. A true Sicilian, she told them nothing. When they asked who had shot her, she repeatedly said "*Unn lu sacciu*, I don't know." The officers departed, along with the doctor who had tended Pietro, leaving Rosa sobbing in one cell and Pietro unconscious in the next.

The jailer was seated at his desk, his back to the prisoners, when Pietro regained consciousness. Through the bars, Rosa whispered to her lover: "Marry me, or I'll tell them you shot me, and you'll spend the rest of your life in jail!" Pietro said "If you tell them I shot you, I'll tell them *you* shot *me*, and we'll *both* spend the rest of our lives in jail." Rosa wailed "My honor is gone! What do I care, if I die in jail?" Pietro blinked. Seeing the logic of her argument, he asked "Will you marry me?"

They were married in jail. Rosa wore a gown made by Maria and Pina. Before the ceremony, Nino managed to sidle up behind Pietro and hiss, "I have no dowry for my daughter. You took her greatest treasure, and you still have your life. Let that be the dowry!"

The next day, at their hearing, neither brought charges against the other, and they were released. Rosina had been stricken deaf in her right ear by the bullet that had grazed it, and Petru would carry two slugs in his belly throughout his life. Years later, friends would marvel at their happy marriage, and wonder: "What was the bond that kept them from ever having a harsh word with one another?"

Chapter 13.

The newly wed (and newly freed) couple went directly to the *Chiesa Annunziata*. While the civil wedding they had endured in jail had legitimized their union and any future children they might have, the sanction of the church was most desired. Like most other couples, they would be married by a church ceremony in addition to the civil one. Nor was it unusual that they would have two different anniversaries, civil and ecclesiastical, although most couples recognized the date of their marriage in church as their true wedding anniversary.

Padre Raimondo spoke the simple ceremony, with only the bride and groom present, along with two witnesses: none other than old Leonardo Avenia and Giovanni Puma! And so those two fine citizens had witnessed the recording of Rosa's birth, her first public act as the *ruotaia*, and now her marriage.

Rosina and Petru went to live in the home of the mayor, and it did not take long for Don Luigi and his wife Donna Susanna to recognize that regardless of her station, Rosa was a remarkable young woman. The mayor, who depended on his clerk Pepe to do most of his paperwork, was somewhat chagrined that Rosa could read and write better than he. They knew that Pietro could have done far worse. Similarly, when Nino saw Pietro shed his shirt to chop weeds at the family *campagna*, after Mass, until dusk, working at it harder than either of his own sons, his anger softened and he quickly grew to love *Pitruzzu*.

But family acceptance was one thing, the disapproval of the town was another. When Rosa went to market, she could feel eyes on her back. She heard whispers and giggles that she took to be about her, whether they were or not. At the pharmacy, customers would stall and avoid Pietro, waiting instead for the proprietor to serve them. When not with their families, Pietro and Rosa seemed to move about the town in a cocoon, either unnoticed, or noticed too much.

Pietro's heart would ache when Rosa fumed "I was good enough to take care of the fruit of their sins, but I'm not good enough to walk among them! My poor child will be looked down upon, and insulted, as we have been. *Iamunnini!* Let's leave this place!"

They spoke with their parents, who sadly but wisely agreed it might be best for them to leave Racalmuto. Don Luigi again suggested that Pietro take a position with his cousin in Agrigento. Pietro responded "If we are to make a new life for ourselves, let it be in a new world. We'll go to America!"

Once the decision was made, the plan moved forward quickly. For several years, as emigration had increased, more and more had become known about the means by which America could be reached. Shipping lines supplied town offices with flyers and posters describing the riches of America, encouraging those who had lost hope for their future in Sicily to come to the new land, and of course, to buy passage on their lines! Steamships now plied the Atlantic, with hundreds and even thousands of passengers per voyage.

Another cousin of Don Luigi's had gone to make his fortune in Buffalo, New York, and he had written that he would have a job waiting there for Pietro. The mayor told Pietro "If things had gone differently, you would have inherited the family home, my business, and possibly even been mayor yourself someday," and he generously presented the young man with notes for a staggering sum of money. "This will be enough for you to make a start in America. There is enough here that you can take a cabin on the ship, and not be stuck in steerage with a thousand other souls."

In the weeks since the marriage, Maria, Pina and even Grazia had labored to produce a hoard of breathtakingly beautiful laces and linens, a 'voyager's dowry' whose worth would treble when the couple unpacked it in America.

Shortly before the couple was to leave, Totò surprised everyone by announcing that he, too, wanted to go to America. True, he was a *picuneri*, but he was tired, not just from the physical demands of the job, but from the mental strain of seeing pickmen demeaned by the mine owners and then taking out their frustrations on the lowly *carusi*.

"My friend Narduzzu has relatives in America. There, they mine coal. It is hard work, but they have no *carusi*. Burros and machines pull the ore out of the mine." Totò did not want to break the family bank, and accepted only enough from their savings to purchase "steerage" passage on the aptly named *Steamship America*, plus the amount of pocket cash required to assure American immigration inspectors that he was not destitute, and a worthy candidate for eventual citizenship.

In mid-December, Totò, Rosa and Pietro were driven to Palermo by the mayor himself, in his fine carriage. The three emigrated to America on the same ship. Rosina and Petru would sail away from the scorn of their community, but with the best wishes of both their families. They boarded the ship and stood at the rail, waving to Don Luigi, knowing they would likely never again see him, nor any of their loved ones left in Sicily.

Chapter 14.

"Who ever knew there was so much water!" moaned Totò to Pietro as they leaned over the toprail on the ponderously rolling rear deck of the *SS America*. Each of them was slightly green. They had been at sea for a week, and several days remained in the voyage. Their sunken, sallow faces and the loose way the clothes hung on their frames were evidence that either they had not eaten much in the past week, or that not much had stayed down.

"I hope we live to see America," Pietro responded, "though I must live, if I am not to be shamed by my wife!" Rosa, in spite of her pregnancy, had suffered neither morning sickness nor seasickness. Instead, she ate ravenously, and took Pietro's portion when he couldn't eat.

Totò was separated from the couple at meals and at night, eating (or trying to eat) his meals in a huge below-decks mess hall, and sleeping (or trying to sleep) in one of the large between-decks compartments that was roped off to mark a person's or family's sleeping space. At night, the only privacy was provided by passengers' blankets or clothing draped over the separating ropes.

Steerage passengers were allowed on deck only for short periods each day. After a week, the odor below-decks was as bad, and the footing as fouled as the worst he had experienced in *Rumpispaddi*. Narduzzu Coniglio, his friend from the mine, was also on the *America*, with several relatives, all from Serradifalco mining families. When below, Totò commiserated with them, and when he was allowed on deck, he sought out his brother-in-law Pitruzzu.

Rosa and Pietro were spared the below-decks squalor because they had paid for cabin passage. They slept in small but comfortable bunks and took their meals in the upper-deck dining room reserved for cabin-class passengers.

But when Rosa heard of the conditions below, she insisted on going among the steerage passengers. For the whole voyage, she could be seen comforting them, especially the children. To the littlest, she would give sweets or pieces of fruit she had culled from the untouched food that had been returned to the kitchen.

As the ship plowed westward, the cold winter wind added to the misery of the sea-sick passengers. Nearing land, some saw snowflakes, a rare sight in the Sicilian towns that were represented on the ship. Finally, as they approached the shore, what seemed to be a giant's figure loomed from the waves. Coming closer, those lucky enough to be on deck saw that it was a huge statue, and were told that it was a figure of Liberty, and that the torch she held aloft was to welcome souls from foreign shores.

Rosa stared up at the imposing American icon that had only recently been dedicated, and the welcoming vision reminded her of the strength and nurturing character of her old friend Anna di Marco. Anna, too, had welcomed the hopeless into her arms. And if Anna could have seen the statue, she might have said that it reminded *her* of Rosa.

The vision dizzied Rosa and she leaned against Pietro for support.

"The voyage seemed to take forever," she murmured "I've lost track of the days! What day is this, Petru?"

"It's January first. It's New Year's Day. At the start of a new year, we come to the new world. And here we will make our new life."

The ship slid quickly past the colossus and was docked at a wharf. It was the debarkation point to the Castle Garden immigration depot, run by the state of New York at the foot of Manhattan Island, in the Battery.

Cabin-class passengers were allowed to disembark first, and were cleared by immigration officers stationed directly on the pier. Steerage passengers, however, were herded into the processing building. It would take hours for all of the steerage passengers to debark from the ship. The growing crush of immigrants from Europe, and the need for more space and resources, would lead the federal government to take over the responsibility for managing immigration, but its Ellis Island center would not be opened until a half-dozen years later.

All the foreign-born passengers, whether cabin class or steerage, were subject to a surprise when they stepped foot on "the new world", for when that step was taken, it landed on an unfamiliar surface – six inches of fluffy white snow. Some marveled and laughed, children shrieked and tasted the stuff, and some voyagers swore that they had been tricked, and that they had been sent to Norway rather than to America!

On the wharf and in the lobby of the immigration building, greeting parties formed by charitable groups tried to make the new immigrants welcome. They presented each family with a small basket containing crackers, cheese and fruit. Here was another surprise. Among the apples and other foodstuffs were long, evil-looking yellow fingers of some strange fruit. Many Sicilians had never seen bananas. The same weary voyagers who had complained about the snow said, "They send us to Norway, and now they want to poison us with these yellow things!" and they discarded the fruit.

After the cabin-class passengers had cleared immigration, they were bundled onto buses, with those from steerage who had not been rejected due to illness, lack of funds, or other disqualifying factors. They went to *il Stazione Grande Centrale*, the Grand Central Station where their contacts in America had said they should board trains to their destinations. Totò was traveling to Pittston, Pennsylvania, where the Coniglios said there was a demand for experienced men for the anthracite mines. Narduzzu and others from Serradifalco were headed there, as well.

Rosa and Pietro had been separated from Totò during the immigration inspections, and now she was frantic that she would not see him again before they went their different ways. She peered around the milling crowd, but could not spot him. She remembered he had said he was going to Pittston, and in a near frenzy, she went up to a ticket counter and shouted *"Pitti-stoni! Pitti-stoni!"* The clerk gave her a frightened look and pointed across the lobby to a large sign – PITTSTON. Through the throng of travelers and commuters, Rosa and Pietro hurriedly wove their way to the Pittston trackside, where they practically ran over Totò.

"Totò! Why are you just standing here? I was afraid we'd never see you again!"

With a carefree smirk, he said, "I knew you'd find me!"

His train prepared to pull out, and Pietro said "You have my cousin's address in Buffalo? Good. Write to us there when you are settled in Pittson." Then Totò's bravado cracked, and he tearfully parted from his sister and her husband, amidst promises to remain in touch.

Pietro and Rosina turned and walked hand in hand to the boarding area for their train. They assured themselves that the trunk carrying their treasure of linens was properly stowed, climbed onto the train, and headed westward to Buffalo.

In their new home, Buffalo, in due time, their baby was born, and in time-honored tradition, they named him Luigi, after Pietro's father.

Rosa was no longer Rosa Esposto, the foundling, nor was she Rosa Alessi, as she would have been called in Sicily. In the American way, she was now known as Mrs. Rosa Castiglione.

There would be more children; another boy, whom they would name Antonino, and girls as well, Susanna and Maria. And sometimes when her children laughed and scrambled about her feet, as her foundlings had done, she could almost hear the sing-song call of the peddlers in the town market, or the church bell ringing Mass. Or the jangle of the chimes of the wheel.

Marquis Book Printing Inc.

Québec, Canada
2012